VÉZELAY

Light and soaring heights

MICHEL NURIDSANY

PHOTOGRAPHS
NICOLAS BRUANT

TRANSLATION
CHRISTOPHER THIERY

Les Éditions du Huitième Jour

CONTENTS

OVERTURE

"Here is the path, go forth", says Isaiah. That is what Vézelay is all about: movement, an enthusiastic surge forward, lyrical standards flying. Pilgrimages, crowds of worshippers, saints, kings, relics galore. Hosts assembling, taking their fill of energy, and then leaving, for Jerusalem, for Santiago de Compostela. Vézelay means a brighter light, a movement.

Observe the immense vessel capping the crest of the hill, plunging through space, separating the winds, the silhouette of a ship on course. "A boat that has anchored on the horizon", to quote Claudel, a frequent visitor.

All around, woodland. The dark, thick woods of the Morvan, full of ogres and fairies and their legends. Forests, and then fields, with the densely-packed fir trees biting into them, and the procession of hills. And above, the great astronomical sky, drowsed with the fume of stars. Lands that are darker than night, rugged indeed, yet with a certain elegance.

Use your eyes, and go and explore the surrounding country: the Morvan will remind you a little of Tuscany, with its civilised curves, the light golden colouring, the church towers that are almost Italian, the quivering landscape. The difference lies in the forest, its sombre, opaque frightening presence, fraught with dangerous spells. An enchanted space into which the poet Chrétien de Troyes sends his knights in search of adventure and glory. At times a halfway house towards elsewhere and dangerous metamorphoses. The forest is the realm of the fantastic, which is familiar to Vézelay.

For Vézelay was born of fiction, of legend, of men's dreams. It all started with the remains of Mary Magdalene, and their "translation" from Aix-en-Provence to Vézelay. According to Patrick Geary, a mediaevalist specialised in such matters, the theft (albeit a pious one) was in all likelihood pure invention … because the relics never were where the Chansons de geste and later reports said they were. According to the tradition that was most commonly accepted in the early days of Christianity, after the Ascension of Christ, Mary Magdalene retired to Ephesus, along with the Virgin Mary and Saint John. In the 6th century, Grégoire de Tours speaks of her tomb, in which one could see her naked body… According to another tradition she repaired to Constantinople; in Provence yet another tradition has her arriving in Marseilles and living as a hermit in a cave at la Sainte-Baume, near Saint-Maximin.

Is this tendency to indulge in flights of fantasy the reason that so many writers have been drawn to Vézelay? Romain Rolland was born at Clamecy, nearby, and died here; the heretical Bataille and Claudel the magnificent came here - perhaps to see Yse once more? Who knows? Vézelay is emotion.

LEGENDS

AND PILGRIMAGES

The invention of the relics

And so it was that Vézelay was born of the imaginary theft of the probably non-existent relics of a saint who was a composite anyway! Vézelay is born of word and legend.

Mary Magdalene, the sinner

FOR INDEED MARY MAGDALENE, as many who have written about this fascinating saint have remarked, is the conjunction, in the Middle Ages, of three Myriams, in other words of three Marys: Mary of Magdala, in Galilee, who has become Mary Magdalene, the sinner who after having lived a "wanton" existence, repented; Mary, another penitent woman who had lived a sinful existence, who came from Nain and is mentioned by Luke (7:37-38), and Mary of Bethany, the sister of Lazarus, who persuaded Jesus to resuscitate her brother three days after his death. The first, Mary Magdalene, was a considerable saint, because she discovered the Resurrection when she went to the tomb of Christ to anoint the corpse, and she informed the Apostles so that they could bring the good tidings to the nations.

BUT FOR THE PILGRIMS SETTING OUT ON THEIR JOURNEY, usually in order to atone for their sins, it was the penitent sinner whom they saw in Mary Magdalene. She was "like a beacon". And Vézelay was said to hold the relics! And they were said to perform cures and miracles!

MARY MAGDALENE WAS WORSHIPPED IN VÉZELAY long before Abbot Geoffroi decided to develop the cult, after Erminfroi de Verdun had built a church dedicated to the saint in 1022. At his instigation, Pope Leon IX issued a Papal Bull making Mary Magdalene the patron saint of Vézelay, alongside St Paul, St Peter, St Andeux, St Pontien and the Virgin Mary. But Mary Magdalene could not simply be a spiritual patron saint, she had to be there physically. And so in 1060 a second Bull recognised the presence of her remains at Vézelay.

Left:
In the light
of Vézelay.

The theft of the relics

IN THOSE DAYS, AS VICTOR SAXER REMINDS US, if someone asked how the remains of the saint were conveyed from Palestine to Burgundy, the answer was simple: "Everything is possible for God", and nobody would express doubt or surprise.

HOWEVER THE MONKS IN PROVENCE COUNTER-ATTACKED, in a verbal confrontation that lasted until the 13th century. According to them, after the Resurrection of Christ, Peter told Maximin to look after her. The two of them, with Lazarus, Martha, Marcelle and Sidonie, were thrown into a boat by the infidels, but with God's guidance they reached Marseilles safe and sound. Mary Magdalene then retired to a cave in the hills of la Sainte-Baume, where she lived for thirty years, until the year 64. Maximin buried her, and over her grave he built a church.

TO THAT THE VÉZELAY MONKS REPLIED that while this version of the facts was correct, in 882 a knight from Vézelay, guided by a divine vision, stole the body of the saint so that it would not fall into the hands of the Saracens, who were ransacking Provence. As this story, however, met with a somewhat sceptical reception, they invented the legend of St Badilon…

THE "TRANSLATION" TOOK PLACE PERFECTLY LEGALLY, because the "États Généraux" (General Assembly) of the province donated the relics to Count Girart, (the founder of the monastery who inspired the 12th century Chanson de geste that bears his name), in exchange for his great deeds in the region against the Saracens. Girart and Abbot Eudes therefore sent a monk, Badilon, to Aix-en-Provence to fetch the remains of the saint. When Badilon reached the town, which was in ruins, he enquired as to the whereabouts of Mary Magdalene. In exchange for some gifts, a few old men led him to her tomb. He returned after nightfall, and found that the body was intact, smelling sweetly. The saint then appeared to him in a dream: she told him that she approved of the plan to remove her from the city that had been laid waste. He thereupon took the body to Vézelay, where he received an emotional welcome.

TODAY WE MAY FIND IT SURPRISING THAT THE VÉZELAY HAGIOGRAPHERS should have tampered with the "original" text of the acquisition of the body in Jerusalem, substituting the story of a theft from Aix-en-Provence (or la Sainte-Baume), which was untrue anyway. In those days however the theft of relics, as long as it was from a devastated sanctuary, duly sanctioned by a vision, and involved mysterious old men, was a kind of spiritual exercise: stories of stolen relics were seen as heroic poems, and were quite popular.

The presence of Mary Magdalene in Vézelay fuelled the zeal of the pilgrims, who flocked to see the relics, said to accomplish extraordinary miracles.

From Vézelay many will leave for Jerusalem and the tomb of He who was nailed to the cross; it is also on the way to Compostela…

A pilgrim's feet

Here we are at the heart of the mystery of the pilgrimages. On the tympanum of the church, Christ in his mandorla opens his immense arms wide: he welcomes you, while at the same time urging you to leave and carry the good word to all nations. His hands emit rays of light… But have you noticed his feet? They are wide, enormous even, under the elaborate folds of his robe. They are the feet of a walker, a pilgrim's feet.

The pilgrimage roads to santiago de compostela

According to the Gospels, the story of St James, the "son of thunder", comes to an end in 44, under Herod: he is the first of the twelve Apostles to die a martyr's death.

THE "GOLDEN LEGEND" HOWEVER TELLS US THAT his body, in a coffin of cedar, was put in a boat which, guided by the Angels (and seven disciples), passed between the pillars of Hercules and was swept ashore in Galicia, at the mouth of the Ulla river. There his disciples buried him, totally anonymously, and he disappeared from the memory of men while hordes of Vandals, Suebi, and later Saracens, overran Spain.

AND THEN IT CAME TO PASS THAT IN THE 9TH CENTURY A HERMIT, PELAGUS, PROPHESIED that the long lost body of Saint James would be discovered; shepherds duly saw a bright star shining above the estuary, and Bishop Theodomir found the coffin. The King of Asturias, Alfonso II the Chaste, built a church to house the shrine of the saint. In memory of the shepherds' star, he called the church "Campus stellae", i.e. Compostela.

A marvellous invention: by the end of the 11th century pilgrims were flocking to Compostela in order to worship the body of the saint, who in the meantime had been credited with having "evangelised Spain". The cult of the relics of the Apostle served to sustain the idea of the crusades and the re-conquest, with James as the symbol of Jesus: the cross versus the crescent!

LEGEND HAD OVERTAKEN LEGEND. The saint became the standard-bearer of a Spain aching to rid itself of the Almoravids and the Almohads, but too weak to do it alone: it had to appeal to Christendom for help and support, and particularly to neighbouring France. It was mainly the Burgundian barons whom the Pope asked to recruit pilgrim-soldiers. From the 11th to the 13th centuries, French knights carried out thirty-five expeditions over the Pyrenees. Cluny provided the link and the cement for putting together these "Crusades". Somewhat later on, when the military - though they were monks - and the "Reconquista" gave way to pilgrimages and worship, Citeaux took over: the Knights Templar guarded the roads, the Hospitallers set up hospices, other monks did road maintenance, built bridges and introduced a rudimentary system of signposting.

Right:
Vézelay,
the basilica,
the ramparts and
the vineyards.

In the hospices, almshouses, hostels, refuges, chapels and hermitages, hospitality was free of charge as long as it did not exceed 24 hours. There were many of these houses of charity, about one every 30 or 40 kilometres, i.e. one day's journey. A guide book, attributed to one Aymeri Ricaud and forming the 5th volume of the Liber Sancti Jacobi, was published by Cluny to help the pilgrims on their travels. In addition to the routes to be followed and the relics that could be worshipped on the way, it gave practical information on the quality of river water, the kind of fish that could be caught, the mores of the local inhabitants and the dangers to guard against. Thanks to the guide book, the pilgrims also knew beforehand at what times sustenance was distributed in the various stopping places on their way, and sometimes even what it consisted of. It is traditionally considered that there were four routes across France to Compostela, from Paris, Le Puy, Saint-Gilles-du-Gard and Vézelay.

vézelay, a crossroads of pilgrimages

Pilgrims from the Champagne region, Alsace, Lorraine and Germany, converged on Vézelay. They were called "jacquets", "jacquots", "jaco-bites", or sometimes "coquillards", after "Saint Jacques" (French for Santiago, "St James") or "co-quille" (a scallop shell, the pilgrims' identifying symbol). Most of them were pilgrims for reasons of personal devotion, but some were there… by delegation. They would be sent by a pious com-munity, or a city, that would have paid travel costs in advance. Yet others were doing penance, of a religious or civil nature. Some did the pilgrimage with their hands bound in chains, a requirement for being pardoned homicide. There were also, masquerading among them, adventurers, spies, deserters, even harlots…

AT VÉZELAY THE PILGRIM WOULD MEDITATE ON THE LIFE OF MARY MAGDALENE who, in the house of Simon the leper, "took a pound of ointment of spikenard, very costly, and anointed the feet of Jesus, and wiped his feet with her hair; and the house was filled with the odour of the ointment. And that is why her many sins were forgiven her, because she had much loved He who loves all men, Jesus Christ her Redeemer". It was said that the relics were miraculous, and let off a pleasant smell when they were touched. They were exhibited on the altars. This worried Cluny, so a saint was found to explain, in a vision, that she would not be able to perform miracles if she were put on the altar, where only the majesty of the divine mystery could be celebrated…

AT VÉZELAY, FOR LOVE OF THE SAINT, SINS WERE FORGIVEN BY GOD;
SIGHT WAS RESTORED TO THE BLIND, SPEECH TO THE DUMB, CRIPPLES WERE STRAIGHTENED,
THOSE POSSESSED WERE DELIVERED, THE FAITHFUL RECEIVED INEFFABLE BLESSINGS.

Above:
It was custom-
ary in the
11ᵗʰ century
to erect Monjoie
crosses in
the vicinity of
the main
stopping places
along the
pilgrim's way
to Compostela.

Right-hand
page: Where
the pilgrims
left from.

THE PILGRIMS WERE MOSTLY HOUSED IN THE SURPRISING AND MAGNIFICENT VÉZELAY CELLARS - some even had fireplaces - that opened onto the side of the hill, and probably also onto other cellars under the houses, which have been destroyed and turned into gardens. The pilgrims shared the accommodation with the farm animals. There were innumerable merchants and money-changers. Especially during fairs and pilgrimages, male and female jugglers sang war songs, accompanying themselves on stringed instruments. They sang in the vernacular the epic poem of Girart de Roussillon, describing in gory detail the mythical battle between Girart, Count of Burgundy, and King Charles the Bold, which took place near the Cure river, and which they made almost as famous as the battle of Roncevaux.

FROM VÉZELAY THE PILGRIMS TRAVELLED DOWN TO VARZY, WHERE THEY HAD THE CHOICE BETWEEN TWO ROUTES: they could either go via Nevers and Noirlac, or by La Charité-sur-Loire, where there was a vast Cluniac abbey, and Bourges with its sixty churches and its cathedral… Then they reached Limoges, Périgueux and the five domes of Saint-Front; next they had to cross the Landes marshes, infested with horseflies. Their next destination was the Roncevaux pass…

The history
OF THE SITE

The "rebirth" of vézelay

In about 858 Count Girart de Roussillon, with his wife Berthe, founded a Bendictine nunnery beside the river Cure, on the present site of Saint-Père. Fifteen years later the nuns were replaced by monks, also Benedictine.

In the beginning: a Benedictine monastery

SITUATED ON THE SITE OF A ROMAN VILLA, the community had access to water from the Cure, to salt from the Fontaines Salées, and to iron from the Ferrières woods. In addition it was well situated on the main Roman road network.

What was even more important was that Girart, considered to be a champion of feudality in opposition to the power of the king, gave his monastery a very special status (the privilege of exemption), and, for better or for worse, this unusual feature was maintained: the monastery was richly endowed so as to be financially independent, without having to pay any dues to anyone (with the exception of a symbolic tax of two pounds in silver to the Holy See), and was placed directly under the authority of the Pope, not the Bishop.

There was a touch of fierce independence in all this which remained long past the days of Girart.

Above:
Ribs spring-
ing from
capitals
(13th century).

On a hill nearby

Left:
The west
façade of the
basilica
merges with
the town.

BUT THEN THE FRANKISH EMPEROR CHARLES THE FAT SPECIFIED IN A TREATY that in exchange for sparing Paris, the Normans would be free to ransack and pillage Burgundy; and so in 887 a band of looters moving up the river Cure laid the monastery to waste. The monks, (and the inhabitants living close to the monastery) fled to the hill nearby, where Abbot Eudes built an abbey, with fortifications. Vézelay was born.

THE "REBIRTH" STARTED A LITTLE OVER A CENTURY LATER, when Abbot Geoffroy, impressed, so it is said, by the prosperity of churches boasting famous relics, began, whether by calculation or a genuine passion for Mary Magdalene, to skilfully promote the miracles attributed to the saint's relics. Crowds began to flock to Vézelay.

In 1104, Abbot Artaud built a much larger Romanesque church; but it was only between 1120 and 1140, after a fire, that the nave was rebuilt in its present form. Pope Innocent II came to consecrate the narthex in January 1132. In 1150, at the height of its glory, Vézelay had 10,000 inhabitants (as opposed to under 500 today, including the neighbouring hamlets). In 1165 however, another fire destroyed the Romanesque chancel and the transept, which were rebuilt in the Gothic style. The nave was strengthened with flying buttresses at the same time.

The crusades

ON 31 MARCH 1146 SAINT BERNARD, IN HIS MONK'S COWL, PREACHED THE SECOND CRUSADE from a podium on the side of the Vézelay hill, where the echo amplified his voice, in the presence of King Louis VII the Younger, his assembled barons and 100,000 knights.

His vibrant tones, his power of conviction and his faith, it is said, fired the enthusiasm of those present, who constantly interrupted with cries of "Dieu le veut! Dieu le veut!" (It is God's will). Nearly all of them took the cross. True, Pope Eugenius III had paved the way for such enthusiasm by proclaiming crusade indulgences for all those who went to the assistance of the Oriental Church. At the same time, King Louis VII, anxious to atone for his sins, had told his barons and the French prelates (who were all very doubtful at the idea) of his intention to go to Jerusalem; saint Bernard, the abbot of Clairvaux, whom Louis had asked to preach the crusade, was waiting for instructions from the Pope... which fortunately arrived at the right moment.

DETERMINED NOT TO REPEAT THE MISTAKES OF THE FIRST, DISASTROUS CRUSADE, the Pope took a certain number of attractive accompanying measures. For instance, the Church would protect the wives, children and property of the crusaders, current lawsuits were suspended until their return, there would be a moratorium on existing debts, fiefs could be mortgaged with churches, if the lord would not accept them…

Eugenius III, who had been a monk under the authority of Saint Bernard (who, may it be said in passing, had drafted the rule of the Knights Templar, had had Abelard condemned, and had refused the papacy in favour of Eugenius III), gave him the mission of spreading his message. Bernard sent a letter to the princes and prelates explaining the Pope's call, emphasising the exceptional grace offered to those who volunteered.

The restoration of Vézelay

"I must still mention the terrible state of disrepair of this magnificent church. The walls are crooked, cracked, rotten with damp. It is difficult to understand how the fissured vault still holds up.

While I was sketching in the church I constantly heard little stones falling and landing all around me. The roof is in dreadful condition. In fact there is no part of the building that is not in need of repair…

Things are getting worse day by day. If we delay in coming to the assistance of la Madeleine, we will soon have to pull it down for fear of accidents".

Prosper Mérimée

Right-hand page: Monks of the Fraternity of Jerusalem

Opposite: The chevet (second half 12th century).

AND SO LOUIS VII SET OFF ON A DISASTROUS EXPEDITION: he lost both the war (with 400,000 dead) and his wife, Eleanor of Aquitaine, who at Antioch gaily had an affair first with her uncle, then with a young Arab. Louis was then made prisoner by the Greeks, and delivered by the Normans! After that he divorced his wife, losing by the same token the Duchy of Aquitaine, which fell under English sovereignty...

AND YET THERE WAS A THIRD CRUSADE, BARELY MORE SUCCESSFUL. And once again Vézelay was the rallying point, for it was there that Richard Lion-Heart and the French King Philppe-Auguste joined forces to once again deliver the Holy Sepulchre... In 1217 Brother Pacific and Brother Louis were dispatched to Vézelay by St Francis of Assisi in person to found the "province of France". The Franciscans have always added a softer note to the forceful, at times even warlike, spirit of Vézelay.

The 13th century sees the beginning of the decline of the church: doubts are voiced regarding the authenticity of the relics. In 1569 the Huguenots occupy Vézelay, ransack the church and destroy the sculptures of the tympanum, as well as some of those in the narthex.

τhe influence of viollet-le-Duc

FROM THEN ON THE CHURCH CONTINUED TO DETERIORATE. In the 19th century Mérimée, who was Inspector of Historical Monuments, discovered the alarming state of the edifice and put a very young (just 26 years old!) architect, Viollet-le-Duc, in charge of renovating it. The Monuments Committee duly submitted a report to the Minister of the Interior in May 1838, and in 1840 the decision was taken to undertake the complete restoration of the church.

In 1920 the church became a basilica, and in 1984 the church and the hill were put on UNESCO's World Cultural and Natural Heritage list.

Today, the monks of the Fraternity of Jerusalem, a contemplative order, have taken over from the Franciscans.

the basilica :

THE BEAUTY OF LIGHT

Like for the town itself, which can only be properly understood after having first walked all the way round it, one should resist the impulse to enter the sublime narthex, and the equally sublime nave straightaway. One should first walk round the immense edifice to get an idea of its impressive proportions.

The narthex: the beauty of light

I DO NOT KNOW IF IT IS HERE THAT WE "UNDERSTAND" THE BASILICA, but it is here that we feel its weight, its size, or to be more precise, its breadth. Of the façade there is not much to be said, because it has been completely rebuilt, which is not the case of the interior of the church. We do however get a glimpse of Mary Magdalene, which is more than can be said of the narthex or the nave, to put it mildly. The Saint is at the feet of Jesus. Lazarus can also be seen, which of course adds to the confusion.

Above:
The upper
windows of
the chancel
(12th century).

Left:
The pier
of the narthex
doorway.

Right:
The feet of
Christ:
pilgrim's feet.

THE ENTRANCE TO THE NARTHEX, AS VAST AS A CHURCH, IS BREATHTAKING. It serves as a transition to the enchantment of the nave. Here, the eye is immediately struck by the extraordinary harmony of the three interior tympana. The right-hand one represents the Annunciation, the Visitation, the Nativity and the Adoration of the Magi; and the left-hand one the disciples of Emmaus and the return to Jerusalem of the disciples bearing the good tidings.

IT IS HOWEVER THE CENTRAL TYMPANUM, a masterpiece that probably represents the Evangelical mission of the Apostles, which strikes us with its strange beauty: the huge Christ, with twisted knees, sitting in his mandorla, arms outspread, palms wide open, emitting rays of light. A fascinating figure.

He is a paternal Christ, exercising his authority in the midst of the agitation of the stone figures on the threshold of the nave, at the passing from darkness to light. The whirling folds of the robes at the knees and the hips, and the way the bottom of the garment is blown upwards, do not detract from the serene, impenetrable majesty of the divine being.

BELOW, ON BOTH SIDES OF THE CENTRAL PIER, THE LINTEL is particularly unusual in the choice of scenes it portrays, with a picturesque procession of the peoples of the world who have come to the Lord, (Pygmies, Panotians with enormous ears), separated in the middle by the enormous figures of St Peter and St Paul. On either side of the face there are cartouches with more scenes in which we recognise men with dogs' heads, (the cynocephalics), men wearing strange buskins, and others with flat noses. Above there are inventive variations on the signs of the zodiac, logically associated with the labours of the months of the year, and with zoomorphic and anthropomorphic subjects: mermaids, curiously contorted dogs in their rounded constraints, acrobats.

Exotic figures. Central doorway, 8th compartment of the tympanum.

Detail of the right-hand pier.

Panotii at the right-hand end of the lintel (1120-1140).

the nave: the soaring heights

WHEN THE DOORWAYS OF THE NARTHEX OPEN ONTO THE NAVE AND THE FRONTAL PERSPECTIVE, we discover the "blaze of the gothic choir": the arches, with their striking alternations of light and dark colours of the stone, are so simple, so elegant. Everything in this great structure is an appeal to light, as is shown by the famous summer solstice alignment of the midday sun exactly along the median axis. Everything in this 62-metre-high heavenwards thrust speaks of liberation, of soaring flight, of a call to the divine.

And the sentiment of praise comes of itself, for here beauty melts into prayer almost naturally.

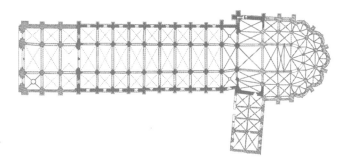

AT THE OPPOSITE END, THE THREE LEVELS OF THE CHANCEL are well marked, although they blend together in the soft light. The delicate shadows of the triforium, between the great arcades, add to the impression of grace and openness.

THE NAVE IMPRESSES BY ITS HUGE SIZE, but also by its peaceful harmony. Everything, in this vast space designed to accommodate enormous crowds of pilgrims, is uplifting.

The capitals: treasures of Romanesque art

THERE ARE 99 CAPITALS IN THE NAVE. Most of them illustrate scenes from the Old Testament. Here we find the "mystical mill", with Moses pouring into the mill the grain of an obsolete Law, and Christ and St Paul collecting in a bag the flour of the message to be conveyed to all nations. Such thinking in allegorical terms is different, not poorer, and perhaps more open to mystery. We also find "Ganymede being carried away", "the Four Winds", "Adam and Eve hiding in the foliage", "the Suicide of Judas", shown somewhat crudely, "the Acrobat", where the geometric representation of the human body is accentuated by the symmetrical separation produced by the edge of the pilaster, and the famous unfinished capital that gives us precious insight into the working methods of 12th century craftsmen.

ALL THE CAPITALS ARE WORTHY OF MENTION, HOWEVER. Even if they are not all of the same quality (several workshops were involved), as an ensemble they give us one of the best examples of medieval statuary, with the extraordinary way in which they tell a story on the three visible sides of a capital, usually from left to right.

MOST OF THE CAPITALS TELL A STORY, and represent the life of saints, or moral or allegorical scenes. The rest are decorative, and represent wonderful variations on animal or plant themes. Only eight capitals are entirely 19th century, the originals having been placed in the sculpture museum.

Left:
The mystic mill.

THE ANGEL
WITH THE HORN,
WHICH CLAUDEL CALLED
"A STONE HURRAH!"

29

*Above: St Peter and St Paul bring
an adolescent back to life;
Adam and Eve, the original sin.*

*Right page, above: Lust; The fight
between Jacob and the angel.
Below: The Four Winds; the Temptation
of St Benedict; St Benedict
bringing a child back to life.*

YES, IT CAN BE SAID THAT, WITH THE CAPITALS AT VÉZELAY, Romanesque sculpture has given us one of its richest ensembles. It will be noticed, perhaps with some surprise, that nowhere do we find, in this extraordinary variety of representations, the slightest trace of Mary Magdalene doing anything whatsoever, authentic or legendary. It is also surprising to find that a third of the capitals are decorated with floral motifs.

A tour

of THE TOWN

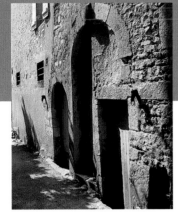

A village of mind and spirit

It is recommended to visit Vézelay on foot. Most tourists do so. But they usually walk straight up to the basilica, whereas the best way to approach Vézelay is to walk round it first.

The path round the ramparts

SATURDAYS AND SUNDAYS BARRIERS ARE SET UP to deter the odd inveterate motorist, although some use their car all the same. This is fair enough, for it is perfectly true that Vézelay should be visited on foot, at a leisurely pace.

Taking the path round the ramparts is really the best way of starting your visit and getting a feel for the town in its setting and of realising just how far back the village goes, because the rue St Étienne does not always show the town's best profile, nor its best front view.

YOU START AT THE BOTTOM OF THE TOWN, where most of the hotels and half the restaurants are clustered together by the main road (N 951) that leads to Avallon via Pontaubert in one direction, and in the other to Clamecy through the Madeleine and the Ferrières woods. You will find the "Hôtel de la Poste et du Lion d'Or", the "Hôtel Compostelle", the "Dent Creuse" brasserie, the "Relais du Morvan", "A la Fortune du Pot", the "Cheval Blanc"…

The Place du Champ de Foire, which was renovated in 2000, is bland and of simple design.

YOU START OFF TO THE RIGHT, WHERE YOU WILL FIND VESTIGES OF THE OLD MOAT that circled the ramparts. Merovingian tombs have been found here. The houses, with their hollyhocks, form a charming crescent, probably following the curve of an ancient defence structure. In the old days the hollyhocks were well cared for, but then they more or less disappeared. They have since returned, with a vengeance, here as all over Vézelay.

Opposite:
The town and the path
around the ramparts
seen from the vineyards.

Next, you skirt the Centre Jean Christophe, to the right of the path, lower down, behind Romain Rolland's house. That is where the "Amis de Vézelay" association holds its meetings.

CONTINUING TO YOUR LEFT YOU WILL DISCOVER THE INTERESTING REAR VIEW OF THE HOUSES, and how they are set against the "eternal hill" (not to be confused with the "inspired hill" mentioned by Barrès, and which is in Lorraine, although here also the winds of the spirit blow). The side stairways are characteristic, forming a wall parallel to the one against which they are built, leading to the gardens that, on this side of the town, are not next to the houses but in a narrow space lower down, in some cases on the other side of the path. We also see some vineyards, which have been replanted recently.

YOU WILL NOTICE BLAISE GAUTIER'S HOUSE; he used to be in charge of the Centre Pompidou's "Revue parlée", a man of great culture and independent spirit, and who possesses one of the deepest and most beautiful cellars in Vézelay.
Now we come to the tower of the "maison des Colons (or Colomb)". This part of the ramparts has been fairly well preserved, for a good reason: people built their houses on top of the old fortifications, with a little garden, and they have sought to keep it all in good condition. We start to see walnut trees, which grow quite well here.

the view of the valley

Abreast of the church, a small steep path leads down to the right towards Saint-Père: the "chemin de la Madeleine". There is a perfect view of Saint-Père, with its 13th century church and belfry.

A Tuscany landscape

BELOW THE TERRACE DENSE BUSHES OF CONSIDERABLE ANTIQUITY completely hide an opening. On the other side there is a magnificent view of the Morvan. In the distance, on a hill, you can make out Tharoiseau castle. At your feet lies Fontette, where you can see the considerable development of the vineyards around Vézelay. To your right, Pierre-Perthuis. Beyond, Bazoches, where Vauban's château is situated. The path then divides into two: one branch climbs up to the Chapter houses, the other slides down to a pleasant little wood where there is a fine linden tree. A little further on, beyond the walnut trees, we get a view of Asquins, the valley, a few vineyards, and the dark woods on the hilltops.

AN OPENING IN THE RAMPARTS, THE PORTE SAINTE-CROIX is just opposite a path that leads to la Cordelle and its 12th century chapel, where the Franciscans had their hermitage. In 1899 a cross was put up on top of two dolmens (quite a symbol!), which is where St Bernard is supposed to have preached the 2nd crusade, on 31 March 1146. On that side the ramparts are in very bad condition, but very interesting, with the 14th century Tour des Ursulines and Tour rouge and their beautifully dressed walls. Enormous branches of ivy and even small trees are growing inside, and will gradually destroy what could still be saved… Everywhere we see fine linden trees, and ramparts in increasingly bad condition, leading to the very beautiful Porte Neuve, where the tourists sometimes park their cars. Instead of repairing the masonry, there are chains to protect them from falling stones. An avenue of walnut trees leads down to the Place du Champ de Foire. A few loopholes and buttresses can be seen.

vézelay, a rebel town

VÉZELAY IS AN OLD FORTIFIED TOWN, encircled by a pear-shaped road system. The Romans called the promontory "Mount scorpion" and its coat of arms boasts a porcupine. It cannot be over-emphasised that Vézelay, while it is certainly a city of the mind and of the spirit, is also a rebel town. A rebel against the established authority, but also against obscure forces that sometimes tried to attack it from within – with no greater success.

We enter Vézelay through the Porte du Barle, with on the left a date carved in the wall: 1814. A pilgrim's scallop shell is carved into the middle of the roadway. This is the beginning of the rue St. Étienne, which is the main street that runs up the whole length of the town, and upon which the houses rarely bother with numbers over their doors.

the life of the town

There are practically no streets in Vézelay, only the one that goes up to the basilica, a few alleyways, and the path round the ramparts.

IMMEDIATELY ON YOUR RIGHT, THE OLD 12TH CENTURY CHURCH OF ST ÉTIENNE, which in 1794 was turned into a cereal market, has for many years been Jacques d'Aubres' tapestry workshop, which operates more or less as a cottage industry. Major alteration works are in progress, there and at the back of the building.

On the left, the "panoramic" terrace of the "Dent Creuse" brasserie, built on the site of a house that was pulled down. A little further up, the Strassard's book-shop, "Le Bleu du Ciel" has become "l'Âme enchantée". Above "l'Âme enchantée" you can just distinguish the faded picture of two billiard queues tied together with a ribbon, with above the inscription: "During the restoration of the church, Viollet-le-Duc used to play billiards in this tavern during his moments of leisure".

Still further up, observe the shop sign "Bazar, bonne-terie, souvenirs, Kodak, photo". Below you will find a heart carved in the stone. It was the sign of an old bawdy-house.

Left:
The maison des Colons (or Colomb).

Right:
The stone hearts above the doors of the bawdy houses.

the houses

ON THE OTHER SIDE OF THE STREET, AS YOU CONTINUE UPWARDS, THE HOUSE WHERE ROMAIN ROLLAND LIVED from 1938 to 1944 is set slightly back from the street, behind a wall which forms a sort of courtyard in front of the house. Building works have been going on for years. Continuing on the same side of the street, you will find "Le Saint Vincent", an excellent wine shop that sells Vézelay wine, but also Chablis, from the greatest vintages to the most humble table wines, and Côte d'Or premiers crus and grands crus.

On the left, halfway up, the house where Théodore de Bèze was born in 1519; it is now a good butcher's shop, that makes a speciality of andouillettes. At the crossroads there is a delightful café ("Le Vézelien") run by Lionel and Nicole Recordon, which serves simple, delicious food, and where you can meet genuine inhabitants of Vézelay, regular customers, and also tourists when a few tables and chairs are put out in front.

THE MAISON DES COLONS (OR RATHER COLOMB), which has been not very judiciously restored, with a strange roughcast on the walls, is one of the oldest and best known houses in Vézelay (rebuilt in the 15th century), in particular because of the inscriptions on the windows and the door: "Quantity less than quality", and in Latin, "I will have ensured that words tally with things", and in the vernacular "As the dove I shall be humble and simple, and my behaviour will be

Left :
The house where
Viollet-le-Duc
stayed.

41

as my name" (colombe meaning dove). Tradition has it that it was through this tower that in 1568 the besieging Huguenots got into the town by surprise.

THE CHURCH OF SAINT-PIERRE HAS BECOME THE TOUR DE L'HORLOGE, opposite the 17th century Friant house, which is now the town hall. Friant was Vauban's steward. A little further up, opposite, there is a 16th century house with a corbelled staircase turret, the Tour Gaillon. On the square, opposite the church, the Sainte Croix house is part of an old Infirmary where Louis VII stayed when saint Bernard came to preach the second crusade in 1146. Viollet-le-Duc also came to the house. Right at the top, also on the square, you can spend a night at the modest Hôtel de la Terrasse, with its little garden, its warm welcome, and its friendly prices. You should also go and admire the two Romanesque houses, one of which is near le Pontot (nowadays a pleasant, three-star hotel), and the other close to the old hospital. But what you will find even more surprising in Vézelay are the cellars, the hidden treasures of the town, and which are not so easy to discover as one might think.

The cemetery

The Vézelay cemetery is a small, "village" cemetery, at the end of the street that skirts the fine Chapter houses, running parallel to the street with an odd name, "rue des Semi Prébendes".

A CHANGE IN LEVEL, ON THE LEFT, DIVIDES IT INTO TWO PARTS. As we go in, we find Maurice Clavel (1920-1979); on his gravestone a simple cross is carved, and a line from the Gospel according to Luke: "I thank thee, O Father, that thou hast hid these things from the wise and the prudent, and hast revealed them unto babes". The next grave is that of Blaise Gautier, and is simpler still (1 July 1930 - 5 November 1992).

TO THE LEFT OF THE ENTRANCE, UNDER A WROUGHT-IRON CROSS, between Louise Maria Scibor Vetch and Henri Vetch, lies at rest Rosalia Scibor de Rylska, widow of Francis Vetch and of John Lintner, in other words the famous Yse of the *Partage de Midi*, whom Claudel had met with her husband and two children on the ship on the way back to China in December 1900, and with whom he had a tumultuous four-year liaison in Fou Tchéou. There is a hole in the grey tombstone, out of which grows a well-kept rose, echoing the inscription behind the cross: "Only the rose is fragile enough to express eternity".

ALSO TO THE LEFT, GEORGES BATAILLE, UNDER A MODEST GREY SLAB. Georges Bataille was poor. A little further on, the Zervos' grave, with on it "Here lie in peace Mrs. Yvonne Zervos, née Marion (1905-1970), and Mr. Christian Zervos (1889-1970), forever united in art ".
Very close by lies Jules Roy, under a simple black cross with his name on it, no date, nothing, no tombstone, just plain earth. Last time I was there, three roses were laid on the stony, slightly raised soil.

surrounding

SIGHTS

saint-père-sous-vézelay

This little village where Girart de Roussillon built a foreshadowing of the future Vézelay basilica is famous for its 13th century church.

THE CHURCH OF NOTRE-DAME-DE-SAINT-PÈRE, that "archangel's arrow planted in a furrow", which Viollet-le-Duc called "my little cathedral", is especially noteworthy for its wonderful porch-narthex and its three doorways in the flamboyant style with a gallery above. A masterpiece of elegance, of delightful audacity, of architectural inventiveness.

And the contrast: just as the exterior is delicate, ornamented, seductive, so the interior is sober, almost austere, a place for prayer and meditation. It is also worthy of note that the outside length of the church, including the narthex, is 50 metres, which is exactly the height of the belfry with its spire.

Abbot Pissier points out another curious fact: everything in the lower part of the sanctuary is 15th century, while in the upper part, from the surrounding gallery upwards, except for a few ornaments, everything is 13th century!

THE CHURCH WAS ORIGINALLY BUILT AS A CHAPEL dedicated to the Holy Virgin. It only became the parish church in the 16th century, with as its patron saint Saint-Peter-in-Chains. Hence the name Saint-Père.

Bazoches : vauban's château

Inside the château de Bazoches, that Vauban was very attached to, you will admire the trapezoidal inner courtyard and the simple beauty of the Marshal's little five-sided study, with its wood panelling and its vaulted ceiling teeming with birds.

"OF OBSCURE ORIGIN" ACCORDING TO SAINT-SIMON'S HAUGHTY STANDARDS, Vauban's family were certainly of minor nobility and very poor when they arrived from the Cantal to settle in the Morvan in the 15th century. Sébastien Le Prestre de Vauban, who has streets and squares named after him and statues in every town in the region, was (most likely) born in 1633 at Saint-Léger-de-Fourcheret. He was married at Epiry in 1660 and moved to Bazoches in 1675. He had been able to buy the land and the château (60,000 livres) thanks to an exceptional gratification from Louis XIV , who was particularly pleased at the taking of Maestricht in 1672 and who showed "great kindness" on that occasion.

D'ARTAGNAN LOST HIS LIFE THERE, but Louis XIV was able to see his young director of fortifications put into practice his system of "parallels", consisting of three parallel trenches linked by zigzagging communication trenches, which enabled the besieging forces to escape raking enemy fire. The attackers were thus able to apply another of Vauban's inventions, the so-called "ricochet" system of firing, which could knock over several canons at once. On this occasion Vauban took the town in thirteen days. He liked to come to Bazoches for a rest during the rare moments when he could get away from the 53 sieges and 140 battles he took part in, and the 333 sites he fortified. Despite his great reputation (there was a saying that "a town defended by Vauban is a town never taken, a town besieged by Vauban is a town taken"), his very considerable merit and the King's favour, he was not appointed Marshal of France until the age of 70.

An independent spirit

Vauban was unofficial adviser to a king surrounded by courtiers, and he terrified ministers with the frankness of his letters to Louis XIV.
The King's reply was: "Continue writing to me about whatever comes into your head, and do not take offence if I do not always do as you suggest".

pierre-perthuis and vault-de-Lugny: two villages on the banks of the river cure

Pierre-Perthuis, built on the banks of the Cure less than three kilometres from Saint-Père, is famous for its Roche percée ("Pierced Rock" hence the name Pierre Perthuis, which has the same meaning).

pierre-perthuis

PIERRE-PERTHUIS IS RECOGNISABLE BY ITS TWO BRIDGES. The largest of them, which spans the valley in one arch, is modern. Contrary to tradition (and to what you may find on some old postcards), the smaller of the two is not a "Roman" bridge, but a pleasing structure built in 1770.
You will find the pierced rock 1 km away; it is a natural arcade 6 m high, eroded by the river in the crystalline platform of the Morvan.

vault-de-Lugny

ON THE BANKS OF THE COUSIN, a graceful river that meanders through alluvial land, you will find one of the prettiest villages in the vicinity of Vezelay.
The village has great charm, with its magnificent 18th century houses. The church is delightful, with its fascinating 16th century frescoes illustrating the Passion of Christ in thirteen scenes, including the Last Supper, Pilate washing his hands, Judas hanged and the devil pulling his soul out.

pontaubert: on the pilgrims' way

In 840 one Count d'Aubert, a brother of Robert the Strong, built a first (wooden) bridge across the Cousin river. Hence "Pontaubert". This was an improvement for the increasing number of pilgrims from Autun to Vézelay.

THE HOSPITALLERS OF SAINT JOHN OF JERUSALEM founded a commandership there (around 1160), a lazaret (a rudimentary hospital for lepers in the middle ages), and built a church.

The Romanesque church is in a late 13th century style known as "transitional", with somewhat severe, but beautifully balanced, lines. In the centre of the tympanum of the porch-narthex a Virgin Mary, wearing a tall crown and holding the child Jesus, gives her blessing to an adoration of the Magi on the left, and on the right, to an Assumption of the Virgin (two angels holding a sheet from which the lifeless Virgin soars upwards, rising to heaven). Among the ancient statues, note the stone Notre-Dame du Saulce d'Island, carved in the beautiful archaic manner.

NOT FAR FROM THERE, AT ISLAND, ON A PRIVATE ESTATE, and visible from the outside only, there is a Templars' chapel, built in the second half of the 12th century, whose territory occupied the whole of the valley on land donated by the local lords. This commandership, which was astride the great pilgrimage route from Avallon to Vézelay, was one the Order's largest establishments in the West. Following the action taken by Philip IV the Fair against the Templars the Saulce commandership was attached to the Order of Hospitallers, which had a commandership at Pontaubert. To the right of the building, at the edge of the meadow, you can see a 200 m. long dike, built by the Templars to contain the waters of an artificial pond, which was common practice in the Middle Ages.

Above:
The church
at Pontaubert:
the vault
of the narthex

Avallon: a city of many marvels

There is a rue Masquée, (a "Masked Street"), an impasse de la Foudre (a "Lightning Impasse"). Towns which have kept street names that speak to our imagination, rather than honouring men whose fame will soon be forgotten are becoming few and far between, and will soon disappear entirely.

AVALLON IS A TOWN WHERE HARDLY ANYONE EVER STOPS NOWA-DAYS, speeding along as they do on the Paris-Lyon motor-way. It is a pity, because on a magnificent site, overlooking the valley of the Cousin, Avallon is full of marvels, with its old houses, churches, and the little museum.

THE MOST BEAUTIFUL HOUSE IS CERTAINLY THAT OF THE LORDS OF DOMECY, with its turret and its outside stairs, which can be seen to the left of the Saint Lazare church.

Next to it there is the pretty Lazare canonical house, once inhabited by André Bocquillot (1649-1748), an Avallon man of science. A little further on, don't miss the 1456 belfry above the new butchers' gate, 9 metres back from the old Roman gate. Until 1772 the aldermen used to meet on the first floor.

You should also go to the Place du Grand Puits (where you will find the carré Barrault with its superb windows), and to the rue Masquée, where there are many old houses, most of them well restored.

THE CHURCH OF NOTRE DAME BECAME SAINT-LAZARE when the Duke of Burgundy, Henry the Great, brother to Hugues Capet, donated to it a relic of saint Lazare - or saint Ladre in popular parlance - which he had received from the Byzantine Emperor. This former collegiate church was witness to the power politics of the ecclesiastical world: in 1077 it was given by Duke Hugh I to the abbey of Cluny and consecrated by Pope Paschal II, who "returned it" to the Bishop of Autun in 1116. The entire church is in the Burgundian Romanesque style of the Cluny school. The triple nave is 12th century. The façade, despite being badly damaged by the Huguenots and the Revolution, is very richly decorated;

it is what attracts people most to this church, although there is also a fine organ, with an equally fine case. To the right there is a Sacred Heart chapel, which has some interesting sculptures painted in trompe-l'œil.

AVALLON WAS AN ACTIVE RELIGIOUS CENTRE FOR MANY YEARS. After the year 1000 however, the influence of Vézelay, with the preaching of the crusades, was such that the little town became nothing more than a stopping place on the pilgrims' road, a shadow of its former self.

Below:
The façade of the
St Lazare church.

Centre:
Cupid running: a bronze
of the Roman era
from Domecy-sur-Cure.
Right: head of young
man, late 1st century,
from the Montmarte
Temple.

THE LITTLE MUSEUM ON THE SAME SQUARE AS THE CHURCH AND THE DOMECY HOUSE is well worth a visit. It contains a number of fascinating exhibits relating to the history of the region (the Ferrières woods, caves, etc.), large statues from the Gallo-Roman temple of Montmarte, near Vault-de-Lugny, and strange paintings by Rouault, in which the influence of his master Gustave Moreau is manifest.

The gallo-Roman
HERITAGE

The presence of gaul

To capture the Gallic past of the region, nothing is better than wandering randomly, exploring the narrow roads and tracks of the rolling countryside, with all the ups and owns left by erosion.

The ferrières site

Above:
The under-
ground
heating system.

Left-hand page:
The ruins
of the villa
probably occu-
pied by the
administration
of the iron
extraction
complex in the
Chaufour
woods.

NOTHING IS BETTER THAN GOING THROUGH THE TINY VILLAGES where the baker, in a small van, delivers bread shaped into those large loafs that have not yet disappeared in this part of the world; or climbing the hill of Saint-Aubin, which offers you a sublime, panoramic view, in particular of the château of Bazoches at the edge of the forest, halfway up a hill; turning back, have a look at the church cemetery, where you will be surprised at the number of gravestones with "Pétronille" on them, a typical music-hall name.

NOTHING IS BETTER THAN GOING IN SEARCH OF THE MEGALITHS that abound, exploring the banks of the Cure or the Cousin, and penetrating deep into the forest, which, according to the specialists, has not changed since Neolithic times. Then you should go to the Chaufour-Ferrières woods, to the Fontaines Salées, and lastly to the Avallon museum, where you will learn much.
The Chaufour-Ferrières woods are on the road to Clamecy just past the Bois de la Madeleine and the Vézelay communal forest. A signpost will inform you of the existence of a "Centre sidérurgique gallo-romain" ("a Gallo-Roman metallurgical centre"), with a picnic site.

TRUE ENOUGH, FROM THE 1ST TO THE 3RD CENTURIES A.D., THIS PART OF THE FOREST was a busy area for iron-ore extraction. Numerous extraction pits have been found, and a villa which probably housed the site manager. There is a porch, a room above a cellar, three rooms with an underground heating system, and a large courtyard. A little further on, the foundations of a small temple have been unearthed, forming a square roughly 5 metres wide. A head was found

there, supposed to be Aphrodite. Hornbeams and periwinkles have grown all around. In the modest museum at Avallon you will find small pieces of wall paintings discovered here, and a stucco frieze with a stylised Lotus flower, like at Pompeii…

THE FERRIÈRES METALLURGICAL CENTRE IS ONLY A SMALL PART OF A COMPLEX that stretched over roughly 20 square km. During the whole of the 2nd century and the beginning of the 3rd, the Gallo-Romans mined an ore called limonite, which they extracted from as far down as 8 to 11 metres. At Ferrières, in an area of 5 to 6 hectares, over 2,000 pits have been found. There are 400 at the "Crot du Port" alone, in an area of 1 1/2 hectares. Once the ore was extracted it was washed in a bath called a patouillet, and then grilled and crushed. It was then mixed with charcoal and flux.

These metallurgical processes required the conjunction of two things in the same place: iron ore and fuel. The Ferrières woods were ideal. In addition, a Roman road (of which the mark can still be seen) passed nearby.

The furnace that was used at the time resembled a small tower of 1.5 m. in diameter. There was an opening at the top, called a "throat", for loading the ore. There were also apertures on the sides fitted with tuyères, made of refractory bricks, for regulating the furnace by adjusting the air intake.

Small quantities of residue can still be found on the site, said to contain metals that could be perfectly well be used in modern industry.

les fontaines-salées

IN A FIELD JUST OUTSIDE THE VILLAGE OF SAINT-PÈRE, in the direction of Pierre-Perthuis, near an old Roman road, the Fontaines Salées is one of the most curious sites in the Vézelay area.

IT WAS RENÉ LOUIS, WHO, WHEN SEARCHING FOR THE RUINS OF THE CASTLE mentioned in the Girart de Roussillon Chanson de geste, first discovered the remains of the Gallo-Roman baths, on the site that is now known as the "Fontaines Salées". Excavations have unearthed hollowed-out oak logs measuring 1.80 metres long and 1 metre in diameter, which served to channel the mineral waters. Carbon 14 tests have shown that the waters were used in the iron age, about 3,000 years ago. It is the only example in France, and perhaps in Europe, of salt water being used in the Hallstatt period (900 - 600 BC). Nineteen salt-extraction pits have been brought to light. In the 14th century, when a salt storehouse was built at Vézelay, the abbot had them filled in. It should be remembered that the extremely unpopular gabelle salt tax was repealed in 1789 only.

ACCORDING TO ALBERT GRENIER: "THE IMPORTANT ELEMENT IN A CELTIC SANCTUARY IS NOT THE TEMPLE, BUT THE ENCLOSURE, WHICH MARKS THE LIMIT BETWEEN SACRED AND SECULAR GROUND".

THERE IS HOWEVER MORE THAN THAT AT THE FONTAINES SALÉES. Funeral urns have been found, revealing an incineration practice of the Hallstatt period prevalent among the Celtic populations who had migrated from the Upper Danube and the Adriatic coast. The term "urnfield civilisation" has been coined in that connection. A circular sanctuary with a 15-metre radius was built in the 1st century by the Gauls, for whom it had sacred healing virtues.

THERE IS ANOTHER 1ST CENTURY SANCTUARY WHERE THE DRUIDS OFFICIATED: it is "T" shaped, 52 metres long, and stretches from East to West. The Gallo-Roman baths, with one hot bath for men and another for women; steam baths; an oven; cold baths and a remarkable underground heating system for the womens' baths, are well preserved. Some of the objects found on the site are exhibited in the little museum at Saint-Père.

It appears then that as early as the iron age Vézelay was an extraordinary centre of attraction. In those days it was not for the sake of the relics, but for the riches of the earth: salt, iron and water. Temples and baths were built all around it.

Below:
The Fontaines
Salées site.

The vineyards

According to Abbot Lacroix, there were vineyards at Vézelay in Gallo-Roman times. Like at Cluny, they developed considerably in conjunction with the activities of the monks.

THE ARCHIVES OF THE CÔTE D'OR DEPARTMENT TELL US that the Dukes of Burgundy owned a vineyard at Nanchèvres, of which the name has survived: "le Clodu" (Le Clos du Duc).

There is also a 1578 document in the Vézelay municipal archives recording payments made to the local vineyard workers. An enormous 17th century central-screw wine press has also been found. In the 17th century there were 800 hectares of vineyards around the basilica... In 1910 there were 1,000 hectares in the four communes that are now AOCs (Appellations d'Origine Contrôlée): Vézelay, Saint-Père, Asquins and Tharoiseau. In those days the Vézelay vineyards were more extensive that those of Chablis.

THE VARIETY USED HERE IS TYPICALLY BURGUNDIAN, THE "MELON" on which Muscadet is based; it does not keep as well as Chardonnay, but it is pleasant, and it put the Vézelay wines on a par with those of Chablis, the Auxerrois and the Tonnerrois.

Henri Garnier, a Saint-Père wine grower, mentions the existence in the 19th century of a "gros-plant". Unfortunately the vines almost completely disappeared at the beginning of the 20th century, with the phylloxera disaster. Encouraged by Paul Flandin to revive the Vézelay vineyards, stimulated also by the growing taste among wine-lovers for local wines, in 1975 and 1976 a few wine growers planted a pilot vineyard of 2 hectares. In light of the success of this venture, other growers joined in, and in 1990 a co-operative was set up. The result is a very palatable wine, which is improving yearly.

In 1988 the Chardonnay and Pinot Noir reds obtained the "Burgundy" appellation contrôlée, the whites being called "Bourgogne Vézelay". There are at present about one hundred hectares of vines on the territory of the four villages.

vézelay

CELEBRITIES

writers and painters

Painters, sculptors, writers and poets have come to Vézelay, fascinated by its atmosphere, both visionary and emotional.

christian zervos : éditeur et critique d'art

IT WAS IN THE THIRTIES THAT CHRISTIAN ZERVOS BOUGHT HIS HOUSE AT VÉZELAY, or to be precise at la Goulotte, a hamlet on the other side of the valley that leads to Asquins. From Goulotte there is a delightful view of the basilica.

Picasso, Giacometti, Brauner, Eluard and many others visited there, both during and after the war. Zervos knew all the painters, all the sculptors, all the poets interested in art. There was a deep and constant complicity between them and this adventurer of the spirit.

YOU HAVE ONLY TO READ THE INSCRIPTIONS on most of the works of the "Zervos legacy" to understand that beyond the message of circumstance, what Picasso, Helion, Brauner, Calder and all the others were expressing was a tribute to the warmth of the Zervos couple, their open-mindedness, their generosity, their enthusiasm.

HERE, REAL OR SUPPOSED MEMBERSHIP OF CLANS, at times antagonistic, was forgotten. Something else was at work, at the heart of a spiritual family formed around the Cahiers d'art, and a little later an art gallery run by Yvonne. More than a school, Zervos, who had a deep, intuitive understanding of art, defended individuals.

Above:
Romain Rolland
at home.

Left-hand page:
Christian Zervos
and Yvonne
Zervos, around
1939.
Behind them,
Nina Kandinsky.

The artists' friend

One day Zervos turned up in Giacometti's studio, while the sculptor was talking with a collector. After a few polite, but brief, niceties, Zervos chose two or three pieces and left, under the horror-stricken eyes of the collector, who could not help crying out "He will never pay you"! Giacometti smiled and said, in his gruff voice: "What does it matter, after all he has done, and is still doing for us?"

Was Zervos a critic, a publisher? He was a man of participation. He created the *Cahiers d'art* in order to have a platform. He adored the art of the Cyclades (he was Greek himself), which he helped to make known. He was one of the first to dare speak of the genius of Picasso, without being blind to other artists who expressed themselves in very different art forms. He was a man of passion, an eclectic, an enthusiast. He liked nothing better than to admire, and to convince.

IT HAS BEEN SAID, I HAVE SAID MYSELF, that at the end of his life he sold some of his best pieces when he was desperately looking for money for his *Cahiers d'art*. He would call a collector, and tell him the amount of money he needed. The collector was then invited to choose whatever he liked in the collection. Even in such a relationship based on trust, and wishing to be worthy of it, the collector did not always chose the worst piece… Zervos donated his collection, which still comprises some fine works by Picasso, Miro, Kandinsky, Léger, Magritte… Louis Deledicq, who had undertaken the task of cataloguing the works, one day came across a matchbox (of the relatively large kitchen variety) with two tiny Giacomettis inside. They are probably the most touching treasures of the collection, which was donated to the town of Vézelay in 1970.

Romain Rolland, a sentinel of the spirit

ROMAIN ROLLAND WAS BORN AT CLAMECY IN 1866. He was the author of *Colas Breugnon, Au-dessus de la mêlée,* and the "Jean-Christophe" saga, which few people read nowadays. He was a lyrical socialist, an avant-garde European, and extremely famous in his day. You could define him as a "conscience on the alert".

"A SENTINEL OF THE SPIRIT" IS WHAT HE CALLED HIMSELF, before the fearsome concept of the "engaged", or politically committed writer had been invented (engaged by whom?). He had length of vision, he breathed widely. He opposed war at a time when war was popular and it was dangerous to speak against it. He fought relentlessly for the independence of the mind, to the extent of finding himself, through his enthusiasm, involved in some doubtful struggles. He was generous, open, curious of everything, with a passion for the theatre and for music; he adored playing the piano, which he did, so they say, fairly well; he welcomed the passing visitor as warmly as his famous friends; it was he who introduced to the world the Indian writer Rabindranah Tagore, and the Rumanian Pamaït Istrati, author of the delightful *Kyra Kyralina*. In 1915 he won the Nobel prize. He had come to live in Vézelay, where "he felt the breath of the heroes", in 1938. He resumed his ties with Claudel, who failed to convert him. He died on 30 December 1944, at the age of 78.

In his house, which in a characteristically fine movement of generosity he gave to Paris University, the only things that have been preserved are the elements needed for reconstituting one room more or less as it was.

georges Bataille: the rebel

HIS GRAVE, IN THE OLD CEMETERY, IS MORE THAN HUMBLE, grey, almost invisible. Even the name is half worn away. It takes a real effort to find it. A plaque put up recently on his narrow little house, which his heirs occupy from time to time, informs us that he once lived there. In fact he lived in Vézelay from March to October 1943, with Denise Rollin, and then from 1945 to 1949 with Diane Kotchoubey de Beauharnais, whom he married in 1951. It was not a period of intense literary activity for him. He did, however, write, or collate, the aphorisms for the *Somme athéologique*.

THE HOUSE, JUST AS HE FOUND IT IN 1943, IS SMALL AND SHABBY, with a long dark passage leading to a dining room and a kitchen with a stone sink. Stairs lead up to two rooms, one looking onto the street, the other onto the valley, with a superb view; Bataille used it as a study. There was no running water, only a pump, and no stove. Wood fires in the chimney were the only form of heating. His neighbours, who probably had never read him, and who are mostly all dead now, are said to have recalled memorable bouts of drunkenness, to the point of catalepsy, and serious discussions in cafés.

THERE IS A FAMOUS PHOTOGRAPH OF HIM ON HIS TINY TERRACE, with a wonderful view of la Goulotte, where Zervos lived, and of Asquins. It was less the Vézelay of mysticism, conquest and crusades that was congenial to this rebel writer – a dedicated follower of Nietzsche when it was wiser not to be, author of *Histoire de l'œil*, under the pen name of Lord Auch, and the magnificent and heretical *Madame Edwarda* under that of Pierre Angélique, as well as *L'abbé C., Ma mère* and *Bleu du ciel* – than the Vézelay of shaggy-haired devils, of which so many adorn the capitals of the basilica, or of the Manichaean heretics who proclaimed their detestation of procreation, but not of the flesh. He himself had founded a secret society: Acéphale, ("I was determined, if not to found a religion, at least to move in that direction" was how he put it). Acéphale boasted a short-lived journal (four issues), illustrated by Masson, and to which Klossowski, Wahl and Caillois contributed. At Vézelay he received his friends, Limbour, Eluard and Nush, Leiris, Romain Rolland, with whom he shared an interest in negative theology. He used to say that literature is only bearable as long as it cannot bear itself.

Marc Meneau
CHEF AND BIBLIOPHILE

Marc Meneau was born at Saint-Père-sous-Vézelay, and stayed there. It is there that he runs one of the best restaurants in France, "L'Espérance". The remarkable success of a man who has remained loyal to his humble origins.

"IT IS THROUGH BOOKS THAT THE PASSION CAME TO ME. You could say that I first went mad on books, and now I am almost more "bibliophile" than cook. But I put my love of books into practice: 98% of my recipes originate in books, and 98% are then turned upside down".

Here is an example: Thirty years ago Marc and Françoise decided to read all of Dumas and Zola, underlining all the words which have something to do with cooking. In "Pot-Bouille", for instance, they find the idea of a tarte aux herbes. The emphasis is on idea, not the recipe itself. The word triggered the process: Marc Meneau began to create his own tarte aux herbes. In his own way. When he was working on the film "Vatel", about Louis XIV's famous chef, he discovered that in the 18th century melon was eaten with salt. While retaining the melon as a starter (it was the 19th century that turned it into a dessert), he conjured up a melon recipe with pepper…

IN FACT, MARC MENEAU WORKS ON THE BASIS OF THREE THEOREMS:
- Marry simple products and sophisticated ones, poor products and rich ones, lobster (or caviar) and potatoes, for instance.
- Marry a product that grows, lives or is reared below zero level (in other words a product of the sea or the earth) with a product of the air.
- Never cook to a temperature above 80°C, for that is when water begins to evaporate, leaving only fibre. It is the water and the mineral salts that retain the taste.

*Specialities
of the house*

Oysters
in sea-water aspic

~

Cromesquis of foie gras

~

Turbot poached in milk

New dishes

Duck-liver quenelle
wrapped in confit
of carrot

~

Warm bone-marrow
with caviar

~

Green olive cassolette
with truffles

Series editor: Évelyne Demey

Art directors: Hélène Moynard, Caroline Renouf
Copy Chief: Reagan Kramer
Engraving: GCS
Printing: SYL

Photographs
by Nicolas Bruant
and
Musée d'Avallon, La Goëlette, G. Leroude : p. 51 ;
Archives Larousse - Giraudon : p. 59 ;
Archives Gallimard, André Bonin : p. 61.

We wish to thank for their availability and trust
Father Daniel Rousseau, Basilica of Vézelay; M. Christian Dérouet, Musée Zervos;
Mme Catherine Buret, Musée d'Avallon.